Reading for Study

A Guide for Students

Sandra Ashman and Phyllis Creme

CW00953477

University of North London

Reading for Study
Sandra Ashman & Phyllis Creme
First published 1982
2nd edition 1990
3rd edition 1993
This edition 1996

ISBN 1 85377 015 9

University of North London
166-220 Holloway Road, London N7 8DB
© 1996

The University of North London is a Charity
and a Company Limited by Guarantee.
Registered in England No. 1000834.

Contents

1
Introduction

Reading is fundamental to all academic work - the way in to the discipline you are studying. It gives you access to the thinking of the thousands of people who over the years have considered the issues of our existence.

An academic subject is concerned with a particular area of human experience and examines that area from a particular viewpoint. For instance, marriage can be seen differently from the point of view of a psychologist, a biologist, an anthropologist, a poet, a theologian, a historian.
So, in pursuing an academic study, we set out to develop the ability to think and describe the world in terms of that approach - to become, in short, a historian, psychologist, literary critic, or whatever.

Through reading, we discover the particular structure of a subject; we learn the kinds of facts that are examined and how these are approached. Although some subjects, particularly the sciences and applied subjects, rely more on practical work than most arts subjects, the written word remains essential to the academic process in all fields of study.

2
Why Are You Reading?

It is important to remember that you read for many different purposes, and it follows that the way you approach your reading should vary accordingly.

The reading you do in your everyday life may, for instance, be different from when you are studying and both involve a variety of skills. You may read a recipe or a set of instructions for immediate application; skim through a page of a telephone directory; run your eyes over the pages of a newspaper to get an idea of the main news of the day; read a novel for enjoyment, or even escapism, as fast as possible to get the 'story', with no need to worry at all about remembering it.

Such skills can also be very useful in academic study - and sometimes students neglect to use techniques which in their everyday lives they take for granted. It might be useful to consider the different kinds of reading you engaged in over the last few days, and particularly to think about the different approaches you used - most probably without realising it - to carry out your particular purpose.

To sum up, in your studying it is important to think about why you are reading and realise your need for a variety of approaches. It can be only too easy to read unthinkingly simply because you have been given a reading list or even because you assume that reading is just something you have to do on your course.

3
What is the Use of Reading?

Most of us tend to feel that the only way to read a book or article is to begin at the beginning and work solidly through to the end. In fact, of course, there are different ways of tackling reading, which will vary both according to the book or article and according to your particular task and focus. Reading is, after all, only the basis of your work; what is important is the use you make of it. The ultimate aim is to incorporate ideas, approaches and information gained from your study into your own view of the world, and to express that view. Only by doing this can you get to grips with your subject.

If you are to make use of your reading in this way, you need to approach it very intelligently and to be prepared to put considerable effort into it.

All students have learned to read in primary school and it is easy to think of it as a skill that no longer requires any thought or effort. However, the fact is that reading is concerned with finding meanings, not just a matter of recognising signs on a page. This booklet aims to help you to make the best possible use of your reading, and help you to approach it in the most effective way for your studies. It does not, however, deal specifically with reading literature, where the form of the work is vital to the overall meaning.

4

What Happens When You Read?

It can be quite illuminating to think about what you are trying to do when you read. Are you for instance trying to remember the facts? Are you trying to pick out ideas for your essay, or to build up a picture of the author's viewpoint?

There is evidence to show that students consistently adopt one of two approaches in their reading: either the 'surface' or the 'deep' approach. 'Surface' readers tend simply to memorise the facts as given without taking time to weigh up their significance. 'Deep' readers are less interested in detailed facts and try to understand the underlying main ideas and the relationships between them.

Many students are able to change their approach to their reading according to the task. If you know that you will be tested simply on the facts, you may adopt the 'surface' approach, but if you know that your assessment will be more of an in-depth matter, you may well, and should, go for a different way of reading, to make sense of the material. In fact, both research evidence and common sense suggest that students who take the 'deep' approach to their reading are more interested in their work, study for longer periods and often do better in their exams as a result, because they are better at understanding their material. If your efforts go into understanding what you are trying to learn, you will be able to remember the details more easily. We remember the series of numbers 2, 4, 6, 8 more easily than 4, 6, 2, 8 because we have developed an underlying concept of sequence in the numbering. Similarly, we can remember the word 'sign' more easily than 'nisg' because we have a concept that these four letters in a certain order refer to an object - they have a specific meaning for us. In both cases, it is much easier to remember the individual numbers and letters if they form part of a meaningful co-ordinating idea. By extension, this also applies to your reading. It is much easier to 'learn' the details if you have an idea of the overall structure to which they belong.

In our reading, of course, we have to go through the process freshly for each new passage, or book, that we read. We learned long ago the meaning of the sequence 2, 4, 6, 8 but each time we read, we have actively to construct for ourselves a new meaning of what the author is saying.

So your aim should be to read thoughtfully and actively; in this way it will be much easier to learn and remember both the author's main ideas and the detailed back-up information.

What is more, if you can really understand the underlying meanings of what the author is saying, you have the beginnings of the next stage in making use of your reading. You will be able to make some evaluation of the author's ideas: to weigh this author's ideas against others; to consider the logic or clarity of his or her argument. Overall you will be seeking to weigh up the author's view of life and eventually to develop your own intellectual position and moral values. We will go on to suggest specific ways of helping you to read more effectively in a later section. First, let us consider a number of different ways in which we read.

Four types of reading
Broadly, it is useful to think in terms of four styles of reading: receptive and reflective reading, skimming and scanning. All types are useful at some stage in your reading.

Receptive reading is the reading you do most commonly, and is close to simply 'listening' to the author - reading takes place at a steady, easy pace.

Reflective reading occurs when you need to think carefully about what you are reading - to analyse, to compare, to weigh up the presentation. You will pause frequently to think about the material. This reading is particularly necessary in your academic work.

Skimming through a text, running your eyes down the page very rapidly, can give you a good general impression of what the material is about.

Scanning a text - as with a telephone directory - also involves running your eyes over a text but in this case you are on the lookout for particular points. It is very useful when looking for answers to particular questions or for specific references.

As an example of receptive reading, some books on your reading list are recommended for 'background' reading. They give you a feel for the subject and a broad context into which you can fit more detailed information later on. It is usually better to do this reading quite quickly and in a fairly relaxed frame of mind; otherwise you might fail to see the wood for the trees, which would defeat the object of the exercise. If a course provides you with a reading list for use before the course begins, this particular approach would be appropriate. Such books might even make suitable bedtime reading.

Reflective reading, on the other hand, is required for books which are virtually text books. Mastering these may be a much slower process, a task more suitable to a time of day when you can give plenty of energy and attention to it. We shall discuss approaches to learning from your reading in the next section.

Another reason for reading may be to find ideas and information for a particular assignment. In this case you do not necessarily need to read whole books; indeed to do so might well get you bogged down in one author's lengthy extended exposition. Instead, you should select carefully, both between books and within them. It is often useful to skim through pages of a book to get a broad idea of its subject, or to scan sections of it to find information you need for a particular assignment. It can be difficult to approach reading in this discriminating way - you might feel you are missing something or that it seems rather a cavalier way to treat the author. All the same, being selective is usually necessary to get your work done and it also forces you to get to grips with your reading and thinking, instead of getting overwhelmed by a mass of reading that you have been unable to digest.

Now that we have considered what you need to read in a particular case and four broad approaches to it, we shall move on to consider what to read; which books, articles, chapters or sections are useful for a particular piece of work.

5
Selecting a Book

When you are faced with a reading list, which may consist only of the title and author with no explanatory notes, or you are confronted by a row of books on the library shelf, how will you decide which book is useful for your particular purpose? In fact, it is easy to pick up something of what a book is about very quickly. This is something you may well do almost without thinking about it, but next time you try to discover the essentials of a book, you might find it useful to bear in mind the following pointers:

1. Look at the title page:

The Sane Alternative
Signposts to a Self-fulfilling Future
James Robertson

This will of course give you the title - but also, in some cases, a sub-title, which may give you further information about the subject matter. The author's name is obviously vital; if it is familiar to you, you should know how useful the book is likely to be.

The date of the book's publication, given on the front or back of the title page, can be extremely important. If it is not a recent publication, the book may be considered something of a classic - or it may have been superseded and simply be out of date. In some subjects, for instance micro-electronics, up-to-date books are essential, because the field is expanding so rapidly. (In fact, in some cases, it is necessary to stick to articles rather than books for up-to-date information). The imprint page should also tell you if the book has been revised since it was first published - this may well make a difference.

2. Look at the publisher's 'blurb'

This often appears on or inside the back cover and gives a brief and useful account of what the book covers; often notes on the author and the intended readership are included.

3. Look at the contents page

This will of course give you an indication of the areas the book covers. It should also help you to see how the author organises and relates the subject matter and appreciate the relative weight given to different topics.

4. Look through the preface or introduction

This should give you a very good idea of the scope of the book and of the author's particular approach. Reading the introduction can help you decide whether to reject the book or it can orientate you in how you regard it.

5. Look up a particular item in the index

Whether, and to what extent, this will indicate to you the author deals with a particular area you are interested in. It may turn out that one or two passages you locate from the index are all you need to read in this particular book.

6. Look at the bibliography

The lists of the author's sources and background reading may be useful for two reasons; firstly, as further suggestions for your own reading and exploration; secondly because the book covers a field you already know fairly well. The author's sources can tell you something about the kind of approach taken and the sort of criteria adopted.

7. Finally, leaf through the book

This will give you a general impression about the book's usefulness. For instance, if you skim through the occasional chapter beginning or end, you will get an idea both of the subject matter and also how clearly it is presented. Look for summaries, which can be useful time-savers, and at diagrams and other visual material, because they often sum up very economically the author's argument.

By now - and this will all take only a very few minutes - you will be able to make some decision about whether to buy or borrow this particular book. Don't get bogged down by reading the book unless it is clearly useful for your particular purpose at this time. You may, for instance, have discovered that you need to read one particular chapter or that this is a useful book to skim through.

At this point, take a book from your shelf and survey it in the ways we have suggested here. Notice how much you can find out in a very few minutes about the usefulness of this book to you and your particular study assignment.

On the assumption that you are now moving on to tackle a piece of solid in-depth reading we will now suggest some ways of carrying out this task efficiently.

6
Learning From Reading

'SQ3R'

Let us suppose that you have selected a chapter for detailed reading. You need to take notes from it which will be useful to you later for revising.

Firstly, remember our suggestion that an active approach, focusing in the first place on understanding rather than mere memorising, is going to be much more productive in the long run.

A long-tried formula, 'SQ3R' is one reading method that many find useful from primary school upwards. It should encourage an active approach and it is quite systematic.

Survey

As with the book as a whole, you can survey a single chapter; leaf through it, look at the first and last paragraphs, and look at section headings.

Question

Before you read, think up some questions that this chapter might answer for you. For instance, what will the author say about 'Fidgeís Theory'? Will it explain what 'relative deprivation' is? As you read on, think up more questions, probably more detailed, and concerned with sentence-by-sentence matters. At the same time, it is useful to try to predict what the author might be going to say next.

If you are not used to this questioning approach, it might be difficult at first. One way of starting might simply be to formulate questions from statements already contained in the book, eg. *The Fundamentals of Human Nature:* What are they? From what perspective is the author approaching this huge subject? These are practical questions but both need some thought to find the answer through reading.

This method of asking yourself questions about your reading is useful for a number of reasons. It helps you to keep your attention on what you are reading, to construct the author's argument in your mind as you read; to relate your reading to what you know already and to what you specifically need to find out.

Read

At this point, and only now, you are ready to start reading the chapter. Aim to read the whole of it - if it is a manageable size - moderately quickly and fluently in a receptive fashion, trying to get an overall grasp of the contents. Don't make notes at this stage, because this would tend to get you concentrating on details rather than on the overview. Also, you can't really be sure of being able to identify the main ideas until you have read the whole passage.

You should now divide the passage into manageable sections, and read each section carefully and thoughtfully. It is best to avoid taking notes at this stage.

Recall

At this stage, you are ready to take notes. After reading each section, stop to make sure you know what it is about and that you can state it in your own words. Now, if you have understood it, take notes, trying to indicate the main points and the supporting ideas and making sure they are not too detailed. (See the Study Guide on *Taking Notes From Lectures* for suggestions on construction and layout of notes.)

Although it takes considerable effort, it is much better to write the notes in your own words. In this way you are processing the information and helping to make it a part of your own thinking which will make it easier both to use and revise from your notes later on.

Occasionally, of course, you will want to include a quotation using the author's own words - this can be very useful provided it is short and not a substitute for your own thinking.

Review
Finally, for the 'Review', check over the process again and skim through the chapter. Have you got the main ideas? Have your questions been answered? Do your notes make sense? Have you now grasped what the chapter is about? The 'SQ3R' approach can be very useful in helping students to read purposefully and systematically.

Try it out on a chapter you have to study to test it for yourself. After you have tried it, you may want to continue to use it, either as it stands, or, with modifications, in future work.

Other useful aids
Another useful aid to learning from your reading is to write summaries of a whole or part of a book, depending on your need for detail in this particular instance. Writing a summary involves two important dimensions. Firstly, you have to extract the most relevant information to get a clear concept of the author's structure; at the same time, you have to reformulate the material in your own words. This is helpful, both in the mastery of ideas and in revising the material later, because material you have produced yourself is always easier to remember than second-hand information.

Teachers know that they cannot succeed in teaching until they have thoroughly mastered their information and put it into their own words. Preparing and presenting a seminar paper is very similar to teaching and again is an extremely useful way of helping you come to grips with your reading; so take as active a part as you can in this work.

Finally, do make use of your fellow students in your studying; students often don't realise how much they can get from each other. Discussing your reading in a small group can be a most effective way of understanding the material and will lead to new ideas being generated. This kind of discussion may take place informally or, better still, in more structured situations. If you set up a group for such a purpose you will find that working in this way is not only extremely useful but can also be very interesting and enlivening.

Remember that it is very important to be flexible in your approach to reading. Fundamentally, you should think of it as a kind of dialogue with the author. You 'listen' to what s/he has to say; you consider it, weigh it up, and are perhaps excited by it. What you read may reinforce, add to, modify or even dramatically challenge your own ideas. Reading should be a dynamic, active process, throwing light on different aspects of our lives. Not all of your academic reading can be as stimulating as this, but it is much more likely to be so when you approach it in an interested and open frame of mind.

7
Faster Reading

The reading process

In the main part of the booklet we have concentrated on the importance of developing a more active and purposeful approach to your reading. Some of you might however also be interested in the notion of learning to read more quickly. This is a technique which many people have found useful, though it is important to stress that speed alone is no use if you lose understanding; you will always have to adjust your speed to a particular reading assignment.

Your reading speeds

As we discussed earlier, you will be reading for many different purposes and it is essential to realise that you should have not one but several different reading speeds, appropriate to particular tasks. Flexibility of approach is all-important and reading everything at the same speed is a sign of a poor reader.

However, the evidence does suggest that most people can increase their reading speed by at least 50%. As well as getting you through the material more quickly, higher speed can also help your concentration by giving more impetus to your reading.

You can try your reading speed on light reading by selecting a passage from a newspaper or magazine. Count the number of words and then time yourself to find the number of words read per minute. Later, when you have considered and practised some of the ideas below, test your reading speed again and see if there is any improvement.

Improving your reading speed

Fixations and recognition span

When your eye moves across a line of print it makes brief, momentary stops. These last only a fraction of a second, but it is during these stops, or 'fixations', when a few words are in sharp focus that reading takes place. You instantaneously perceive and recognise one or at most two words. A further three or four may be blurred but distinguishable enough for you to fill in the general meaning.

The number of words recognised at each fixation are said to be 'within your recognition span'. The extent of this recognition span is one of the factors which vary considerably between the slow and the fast reader.

You can test your recognition span by looking at a line of print. Maintain your fixation on the second word along and see how many words you can see to the right and left of it without moving your eye. You will probably see two or three words clearly and have a vague impression of one or two more. Your aim should be to increase this recognition span to give five or six words, and you can practise this by stopping on every fourth word on the line. In this way you will make fewer fixations per line and speed up your reading.

In addition to extending your recognition span, you should attempt to reduce the time between fixations. Try to develop fast and rhythmic eye movements, keeping the head and shoulders as still as possible.

Good lighting is important if you want to speed up your reading. Eye problems can also adversely affect your reading, so you should have a regular eye test and wear any glasses you have as prescribed by the optician.

Speeding up

Another way of forcing your speed is to take a piece of paper as a guide and move this down the text, gradually speeding up, making your eyes move more quickly down the lines of print.

There is a strange paradox to reading more quickly! Very often quite considerable improvements can be made just by having the confidence that you can read more quickly. Of course your brain can only process the information at this higher speed if you are familiar with the language and content of your text. A new expression or a complex formula will inevitably and correctly slow you down as you spend longer looking at it and considering its meaning.

Sub vocalisation

Most of us learn to read in primary school by reading aloud to the teacher, slowly and carefully. This may be the cause of another bad habit which slows down many readers. As you read, place your finger on your lips and you may well find they are moving. This talking to yourself, or sub vocalisation, makes it impossible for you to read at much more than 120 words per minute, the average speaking speed. So make a conscious effort to read so fast that you cannot 'sub vocalise'.

Regression

'Regression', or the habit of going back to check your understanding, can considerably reduce your speed. It can also result in your losing much of the meaning of the sentence or paragraph. Again, confidence that you are understanding is all important. If you know your purpose in tackling a text, as we discussed in earlier sections, you are less likely to feel the anxiety which makes you regress and waste time.

Of course, sometimes you do have to go back and check the meaning of something; it may be a very difficult text, or just poorly written and badly organised. Even then it may be better to read the whole passage through twice at a rapid speed rather than one long slow read.

Almost all students who attend a speed reading course do make a significant improvement in their reading speed. Bearing in mind the points made in this supplement about faulty eye movements, regression and sub-vocalisation, try a systematic approach to improving your own reading speed.

Spend 10-15 minutes a day practising reading more quickly. This could yield very worthwhile results over a period of three to four weeks. Choose your own material but keep it similar in type. Read as fast as you can without losing comprehension.

After this period, test your reading speed again and see what improvements you have made.
You may well find that it has considerably improved.

Further Reading

Buzan, T., Use Your Head, BBC, Chapter 2.
Rowntree, D., Learn How to Study, MacDonalds, Chapters 3 and 5.
Webster, O., Read Well and Remember, Pan.

Other Study Guides available from Blackwell Bookshops

Taking Notes from Lectures

Your notepad's out, your pen's at the ready, but can you convert the stream of words you hear into a form that will be of use to you afterwards? How often have you turned back to old lecture notes to discover a mass of unconnected phrases whose importance you can no longer remember? This handy pocket guide gives clear, concise advice on what to look for in lectures, and how to put it down efficiently for easy recollection and revision.

How to Write Essays

You may have all the facts at your fingertips and be brimming with theories and explanations, but are you doing yourself justice on paper? Giving help at every stage of the essay, from interpreting the question to the final follow-up, this handy pocket guide gives full, clear, concise guidance both for those who are tackling essays for the first time, and those who suspect that they could write them better.

Blackwell Bookshops
50 Broad Street, Oxford OX1 3BQ